State of the Ummah

A Muslim Poetry Collection

S. H. Miah

Muslim Fiction Project

Contents

The Patient

We are all sinners

In our own private worlds,

Toying with vice with a whirl,

Like trampolines when we finally come down,

Back to the sinner's high we all feel.

But Allah's truth will always be revealed.

We cannot continue forever,

Except in eternal pleasure or pain.

This world is fleeting, depleting

Our life with every second in vain.

Allah's Prophet (SAW) came with the message

To the sinners amongst mankind,

Of guidance from the Lord Most High,

A Lord we forget except in hard times.

A Lord always there, in our struggle and strife.

Waiting for us to call Him with words of regret,

Repentance of sins remembered and sins we forget

He is always waiting for us, The Patient.

Us sinners must not be stuck in conflation,

Between the high of sin and the bliss of salvation.

Allah is The Patient, but he will not wait forever for your repentance. Are you delaying it? If so, why? What are the consequences of this?

Think, O Muslim, O worshipper of Allah. Think.

Al-Qur'an

Al-Qur'an.

Allah's Speech.

Muslims, take heed.

Your lives are wrought

With an utter imbalance of

Justice. Towards yourselves. From the whispers

That Satan thirstily plants in your ears.

Al-Qur'an.

Allah's Speech.

Muslims, please read.

Your salvation is within

The holy Word you ignore

For distractions that surely blind you

To the eternal paradise calling its seekers.

Al-Qur'an.

Allah's Speech.

Muslims, ponder carefully.

The Miracles of Allah

Are vast in the universe.

Waiting for remembrance, waiting for contemplation.

So look, to the Book, then stars.

Al-Qur'an.

Allah's Speech.

Muslims, go forth.

Spread in the land.

Drinking from Allah's endless blessings.

Thirsty for more, which are given.

Yet your hearts yearn that which displeases.

Al-Qur'an.

Allah's Speech.

Muslims, take note.

With deep, devoted reminiscence.

The days in the womb.

In utter darkness, fed by Allah.

A state wherein none else can provide.

Al-Qur'an.

Allah's Speech.

Muslims, come forth.

Dishevelled, dusty, dampened, disheartened,

With dua your only weapon.

Come, beg the Lord that feeds

Yourselves and your families, your entire world.

Al-Qur'an.

Allah's Speech.

Muslims, take pride.

You have been gifted.

With mankind's greatest, perfect example.

Follow what was revealed to him.

Study. Reflect. Surely, Allah's Mercy will descend.

What is our relationship with Allah's Speech? Do we read it on a daily basis? Do we merely recite it, without heeding the guidance it gives us through pondering its meaning?

Just a few things to think about.

O World!

O world!

Why do we sacrifice everything for you?

Do you give us life?

Death?

Providence?

Success?

What do we seek with you?

Why do we lust after what gives us

Nothing in return?

At the end, we shall return

To the Lord that created us.

Fashioned us.

Blessed us.

Gave us

The ability to thirst after these illusory delights.

At the end, our abode is not on the world,

But under it.

And our sacrifices

Have cost us the world we should have been striving for.

Assess your effort levels when working for the dunya and compare it with work for the akhira. Do you put more effort in your job, but your prayer is lazy? What are you really after? This life, or the next?

O Jannah!

O Jannah!

Your delights call to us.

The sweetest of honey

Flows through your valleys,

In rivers and streams,

Their noise unimaginable to the mind.

Wine, the taste indescribable, that does not

Render its drinkers drunk.

Fine it is as a substitute for the impermissible.

Gardens bristling with creations beyond this world,

Housing springs and shrubbery without painful thorns,

With pearl and green for your inhabitants to adorn

Their youthful bodies, and not a scorn

Will sully the faces of the successful.

Depression, sadness, all ailments of old

Not present within your palaces of gold.

Milk runs through you in its purest essence,

Delighting the dwellers with its musky taste.

A fragrance unlike any air freshener

Encompasses, eternal, and never to waste.

Fruits that grow better with every bite,

With meats that impress a limitless delight.

An eternal shade, an eternal bliss.

But are we doing enough to earn this?

Are we doing enough to earn this?

Many of us love to read about Jannah, and read about the delights the successful ones will experience. Yet, do we ever

ponder whether we will be gifted these pleasures in the first place? We look forward to the afterlife, but what have we prepared for it?

A Banana's Peel

A banana's peel

Is not what we seek.

Its true essence,

Is the sweetness inside.

Beautify your within.

Then, regardless of the peel,

You will flourish.

A beautiful heart and a beautiful character far outshines any outer beauty one can plaster onto themselves.

O Youth!

O youth!

Your preoccupations are with

That which does not sustain you.

You swim in hedonism with

Constant backstrokes.

Moving, yet to where?

O youth!

Your free time is an ocean

Lapping at the shores of

Productivity. Yet only small

Tides come forth.

Progress, but to where?

O youth!

Your energy is like thunder crackling with

Potential in every motion.

Lightning, yet only small

Shocks come forth.

A taser with no trigger.

Our youth is when free time is the greatest, but we find laziness at its height in these formative years, too. Let us battle the laziness, and not waste these precious moments, such that we look back and realise our youth has accounted for nothing in this life and the next.

Body Parts

Shrapnel fills our streets

Like a child's packet of Eid sweets.

Fumes spill into our windows

Like foam splitting from pillows.

Howls fill our ears,

Like it is all we can hear.

Gunfire booms outside,

Like thunder in the sky.

We scream, we cry out,

But can anyone hear our shouts?

We are the bleeding body parts

Whose wounds are still yet open.

Are we doing enough to help those in need?

Regret

You go to the grave,

See the name, of the parent you once

Verbally lashed with a voice laced

With unbridled hate, a hit worse

To them than even a mace.

And now, you pray, for Allah to erase

Their sins, their shortcomings, preserving their grace.

Their face shines in your mind,

It creates a smile on your face,

As you reminisce.

Then regret the harshness you dealt them,

And you wish,

For a second more,

To apologise,

And embrace.

Do not oppress one's parents. Indeed, a time may arrive wherein seeking their forgiveness is no longer an option.

We Cannot Capture

Light, emanating,

From the heavens,

Lighting the world,

With a grace we

Cannot capture.

Are we doing enough to attain Allah's Mercy?

Allah's Mercy

Allah's mercy descends, waiting

For sinners to clamp onto

Repentance, and drink from that mercy,

Like it is a fountain of heaven,

Flowing freely with no end.

Again, are we doing enough to attain Allah's Mercy?

Three Sixty Five, Seven Twenty Four

Three sixty five,

Seven twenty four.

You are being called,

Like a knock on the door.

Like a buzz on your phone,

A melodious ringtone,

Wafts through your home,

Inviting you into the Mercy

of The One, who, Alone,

Is worthy of worship

And Worthy of praise,

But instead we seek help,

From those with no might,

No power to assist,

Except with the Will

Of the One who calls us.

Three sixty five,

Seven twenty four,

And yet, after all His calls,

We still, in ignorance, ignore.

Allah is calling us, in every minute of every day. And yet we still find it hard to pick up.

Why?

Dua is the weapon

Dua is the weapon of a believer.

Like the sharpest knife,

The blade cutting through life,

Like a saw through oak,

Dua is the front stroke,

Pushing believers through

The ocean of dunya,

Teeming with sharks and piranhas,

Coral reefs dazzling, a distraction

From the end destination,

On the horizon,

Which bends to the stars,

Because, ultimately, heaven

Is where dua can take us,

If only we are faithful enough

To wield it.

Dua can move boulders, shake mountains, split the sea.

And yet dua is, in our lives, an absentee?

The Heart is a Fickle Being

The heart is a fickle being.

It hurts with a whimper,

Roars like a lion,

Claws at one's chest,

Soars like it's flying.

The heart is a fickle being.

It burns with a flame so

Bright yet like a flash of thunder.

Temporary, fluctuating up

And down like a Holter monitor.

The heart is a fickle being.

It yearns for this dunya

With a desire like the starving

Bird's hunger to feed its children,

But the heart only feeds itself.

The heart is a fickle being.

But deep inside its recesses,

It requires a remembrance we seldom

Provide, of The Ultimate Provider. Only

Then will the heart be at rest.

Do we nurture our heart, tend to its wounds?

Or do we let it be attacked, burned to ruins?

The one who cares

You've been out all night, worry to the wind,

Smoking it up with some of your friends,

Loitering about, not a care in the world,

When the one who cares the most sits on the bend

At the bottom of the stairs, knees tucked in,

Eyes wide shut, lips almost burst in,

Scarf wrapped over her neck, wet with tears.

Then you enter your home, with blood on your ears.

Just another fight, that's what you say,

Not letting embarrassment hold any sway

Over the lies that you spew, countless lies

Before the only one who cares about you.

Just another fight, yet it was anything but.

A gang beef, one turf against the other.

Postcodes clashing, lives colliding,

With death and destruction, one after another.

Your heart is plunged with a groping sadness,

And that one who cares asks what happened.

You shrug her off, eyes averted

Nothing's the problem, so get out of my space.

Disjointed, troubled, you're back outside

And smoke up another packet as you ride

To the lads, chilling by the park corner,

Weed in their hands, rolled and primed.

What happened to Johnny, that's what you ask

And they stare blankly, since the weed has masked

Their minds, their eyes, as if they cannot see,

Johnny's gone, mate, but do you like this whip?

Your mind feels whipped as you head home again,

Johnny just died, but no one cares.

But then you realise, someone *is* crying for Johnny,

Like the one who cared about you all along.

Johnny has a mother, and a family he held

Dear to his heart, and then he left them

Without a son, a brother, a friend,

And the one who cares about you sits at the bend

At the bottom of the stairs, and her face is blotched,

Tears roll down both your faces, and you enter,

And you promise, three times, never to return to your ways,

And you give her a hug, basking in her grace.

When was the last time you gave the one who cares a hug?

If they aren't around anymore, why not make a special dua for them?

Sins are players of Jenga

Sins

Are players of Jenga.

The greater our sins,

The less blocks we have,

Until our whole life

Crashes.

How close is your game of Jenga to crashing?

The Sanctity of Nature

The sun and the moon,

The stars in the sky,

Each white dot,

Signifying an orbit,

As Allah ordained.

And we have a choice,

And choose, to disturb

The sanctity of nature.

Nature is perfectly fine-tuned.

Are we disturbing the balance?

Keeping up with the Ahmed's

Ahmed's got a new car.

Seven seater, massive boot.

He's got another one, you know,

Lambo, speed like a bullet's shoot.

Ahmed's got a new house.

Six bedrooms, large kitchen,

Dining room fit with a furnish,

Two bathrooms, attic built-in.

Ahmed's got a new TV.

Seventy inch, flat screen,

2K to 4K Ultra HD,

The smartest TV ever seen.

Ahmed's got a massive garden.

Grows his own fruits, plants

Roaming the edges, an array

Of colours he has, but we can't.

Ahmed's a banker.

High-paying job. Cash

In racks upon racks,

Hauled into a massive stash.

But what we don't see,

Is that Ahmed, in all his luxury,

Finds no semblance of peace,

Not even within the gold-plated cutlery.

So don't keep up with Ahmed.

Jannah is in the heart.

And it may well be, that following Ahmed

Causes you and Jannah's paths to part.

That new item you buy—are you merely following a trend?

If so, are you truly happy?

Like Suns

Mothers

Are like suns.

Every morning

They rise, and

The world fills

With light.

Again, when was the last time you gave your mother a hug?

If they aren't around anymore, why not make a special dua for them?

Did you hear about the murder?

Did you hear about the murder last night?

Was it a terrorist?

No, it was a white man, English,

With a bit of stubble and a

Hole in his heart.

Depression, they said,

Said the man suffered for years.

Suffering that built

Til he decided to kill,

And caused unmeasurable tears.

What about the other murder a week before?

Yes, it was on the news this morning.

A terrorist, thick beard, long gown,

Islamist, dodgy twitter account,

Suffered from depression

But you know what they'll lie about.

Got divorced a few weeks before the murder,

The anger probably made him kill.

I'm joking, that sounds preposterous.

It was, of course, his religion.

Because, when they're Muslim,

That's all we can see in them.

Is he a terrorist because he caused terror?

Or is he a terrorist because he's a Muslim?

That Twinge

There's a twinge that accompanies

An apology spoken,

A twinge in the chest.

So wronged are we, to assume

Allah requires our apology.

We require him,

In a way unrequited.

That twinge must be filtered

With the sieve of remembrance,

Filtered, until the heart is broken,

Once more ready to meet its Lord.

*Can we overcome that twinge and truly apologise to our
Lord for our wrongdoings?*

Identity

When you look at yourself,

What do you see?

A beard? A scarf?

A true identity.

Wear it proudly.

For that chiffon bears the

Responsibility, of 1400 years

Enriched with history.

And those hairs on your chin,

Despite how small,

Carry the way of the

Best example of all.

That thobe you wear

Shows everyone your deen.

And the abaya that hides

Beauty with every seam.

Let the mocking come

Till dusk meets with dawn.

Our pleasure lies with Allah's,

On a day in which the scorn

Of those mocking ones

Will turn to hideous shrieks,

Wishing they were never born.

Do not be embarrassed by your identity. Wear it proudly.

For, indeed, therein lies Allah's bounty.

Shaytan is like a dog

Shaytan is like a dog,

Licking its lips, salivating

When another marriage breaks down

Through misunderstanding, and disobedience

Of Allah's command.

Shaytan is like a dog,

Licking its lips, salivating

When a father fails to bear

The duty to his wife and child, and leaves,

Disobeying Allah's command.

Shaytan is like a dog,

Licking its lips, salivating

When a mother shackles her child, away

From a loving father, in disobedience

Of Allah's command.

Shaytan is like a dog,

Licking its lips, salivating

When a son, a daughter, disrespects

The parents to which they are indebted

Like the leaves are to the sun.

Shaytan is like a dog,

Licking its lips, salivating

When mankind hears his whispers

And acts upon sinful impulse. An ultimate

Disobedience of Allah's command.

In the end,

Shaytan bears less fault

Than the sinner,

And we are left with the chains

Of our destruction.

Shaytan is like a dog. But definitely not one you wish to play with.

That's all it was

Spilt milk.

That's all it was.

Old silk.

That's all it was.

New ilk.

That's all it was.

Strong will.

That's all it was.

Late bill.

That's all it was.

Steep hill.

That's all it was.

Climb still.

That's all it is.

We chose the way out.

The kids are still suffering.

Are we breaking apart too easily, without good reason, and causing those around us to suffer immensely?

One Body

An arm is flailing, both broken and ripped.

The ribs are failing, overworked and under siege.

The brain is collapsing, stretched beyond limits.

A leg's been chopped, chopped into bits.

A foot has been cut, the second to follow.

A hand is gripped, bones crackling when snapped.

The other is chipped, tired, and cracked.

A thigh is burning, engulfed with tomorrow.

The back is waning, under the weight of the knocks.

The chest is paining, with bloodshed the cost.

Ears bleeding, eyes leaking, nose utterly blocked.

The ummah, one body, suffering from loss.

The ummah is one body, a body suffering from loss.

May Allah strengthen us, Ameen.

Iman Airlines

Iman Airlines.

A strange little plane.

I totter up the steps,

Then begins the race.

Luggage scanned. Cutlery banned.

Then I saunter to the gates.

Get through, not a terrorist.

I travel alone. Without mates.

I board the plane. Yawn, then wane.

Look out the window as takeoff claims

The engines, which rumble like thunder in the rain.

Clutch onto my seat, back in pain.

Out the window again, I see the world smaller.

Fields and streams flow into one another.

Stalks and beans that once seemed so taller

Than the sinful earth that now begs back its caller.

Iman Airlines.

A strange little plane.

The higher you go,

More the world feels in vain.

If you find yourself attached to this world too much, nurture your iman. Indeed, your love for the dunya will naturally lessen.

The Carousel

The Carousel

Goes round and round,

But who can tell

Of the Carousel's delights?

A mystical unicorn,

Horn so long,

With a spiked tail of sorts,

And a mane plastered on.

A blown up cone

Dolloped with ice cream,

Dripping, dripping,

So the sweetness creeps in.

A terrifying lion,

Roaring with a grin,

Claws that can kill,

And tear flesh from within.

A large loveseat,

Nicely fit for two,

Swings around The Carousel,

Hunting for you.

A globe, all round,

Swings up and down,

A face painted on,

Turning from smile up to frown.

The Carousel

Goes round and round,

But in the end,

It goes nowhere.

You return to

Where you found.

Is your life like The Carousel? Filled with events, yet in the end you get nowhere?

Life is a Clock

Tik Tok.

Our life is a clock.

Ticking til the day comes,

Where we all flock,

Back to Allah.

Our lives, that day, will play

Like a film reel,

And we will be questioned,

As to why we wasted our precious,

Minutes, seconds,

Every Tik Tok,

On TikTok,

On our screens, with the false

Belief that we find pleasure

In scrolling. When, in fact, our

Brains are dead, dishevelled, unkempt,

A rotting corpse of anxiety and dread.

But the screens did this to us, right?

On the Day of Judgment, let's see

If that excuse can carry our plight.

*How many hours a day do we waste on screens? How many
precious moments do we miss?*

Ocean of Knowledge

Waves of the ocean rock your toes

As you step on the edges of the beach.

You reach out, arms wide, as if to grab the water

That with every second, gone by, recedes.

You smell, like garbage, arms rotten and weak.

Can't tell, light headed, how badly you reek.

The ocean swirls, and stomps, nearly a speak,

Begging you, to go bathe, wash out the weeds.

But you refuse, why? Because the beach is retreat,

With ice cream stands and beautiful sand, all at your feet

With laid back chairs and cushiony fairs, delicacies to eat,

Long palm trees, with stalks and leaves, sway in deceit.

An ocean of knowledge removes the worst of your sins,

The rotting dirt, with filth, that sullies your skin.

Step forward, toes first, dip them right in.

Then bask, in the blessings, from the ocean's within.

How can we expect to improve our lives without having the knowledge to do so?

Worth it, in the end

Lego litters the floor.

A bundle right by the door.

Hpmh. There's another chore.

I pick up. Put back. Then hear a roar.

I rush out, panic seizing my heart.

Then see a hideous work of art.

Paint spilt all over the tiles with a mar.

I wipe. I clean. Then rumbles in a car.

Toy cars, all broken and snapped by the head.

The metal pieces like shrapnel instead.

I walk over, rife with tingles of dread.

I pick up. Put back. Hear the creak of a bed.

I instantly run, corner the bend

At the bottom of the stairs, reach the top, and then

I open the door, sneak in, and send

Stares to the source of all troubles without intent.

But he's my child. I'm his mother.

And it's worth it, in the end.

To all the mothers of the world, you are valued and precious.
What you do can never be accounted for.

State of the Ummah

What's the state of the ummah?

A question seldom asked.

We think of ourselves, every day,

With every waking moment,

With every breath.

Outside, others live, in our peripheries,

Their lives just as existent

As ours.

Yet our hearts

Never extend beyond ourselves,

Or those we claim to love.

But what is true love,

Except loving for your brother

What you love for yourself?

Faith is what binds us.

Iman is thicker than blood.

Faith runs through our veins,

Jugular and close,

Deeper than the recesses of our heart,

Heavier on the scales than

A dunya of good deeds without it.

And yet, our hearts are shackled,

Constrained,

Locked.

Enraptured

With ourselves are we,

When the ummah is but one body,

And we are but a pore,

Relying on the heart of faith,

To survive, in this world and the next.

So don't look past the ocean for the horizon,

For indeed both are not blue,

Except for an illusion.

Look to the stars, the heavens,

Because indeed, in those gardens,

The state of the ummah will be pure,

Whole,

Like it once was.

Afterword

This is my first foray into writing poetry. Hopefully, it lived up to the title.

The state of the ummah is a concern we should all have in our hearts, especially as our brothers and sisters are suffering across the globe. Especially in the English-speaking world, many of us live our lives heedless of the struggles the ummah faces.

Identifying those struggles helps cause change.

I hope this poetry collection aided, in at least some way, towards that.

Jazakallahu khairan for reading,

S. H. Miah

About MFP

The Muslim Fiction Project, MFP, is an initiative started by S. H. Miah to publish works of fiction that promote Islamic messages for Muslims all around the world.

Written for Muslims. By a Muslim.

Visit our website to see what other stories you could sink your teeth into!

About S. H. Miah

S. H. Miah is the founder of Muslim Fiction Project. An initiative to produce high-quality Muslim fiction. Written for Muslims. By a Muslim.

When not writing, S. H. Miah enjoys spending time with family and friends, charging through his own reading list, and of course having a bit too large an obsession with spiral-bound notebooks.

For more information about Muslim Fiction Project, please visit: https://www.muslimfictionproject.com